*Holy Places*

# Bodh Gaya

## and Other Buddhist Holy Places

Mandy Ross

For information, address the publisher:
Raintree, 100 N. LaSalle, Suite 1200, Chicago, IL 60602

Design by Joanna Sapwell and StoryBooks
Printed and bound in China.

07 06 05 04 03
10 9 8 7 6 5 4 3 2 1

**Library of Congress Cataloging-in-Publication Data**

Ross, Mandy.
  Bodh Gaya / Mandy Ross.
    p. cm. -- (Holy places)
Summary: An introduction to Buddhism which focuses on Gautama Buddha and
on holy sites of the religion.
Includes bibliographical references and index.
  ISBN 0-7398-6077-1 (HC), 1-4109-0050-9 (Pbk.)
  1. Buddh Gaya (India)--Juvenile literature. 2. Gautama
Buddha--Juvenile literature. [1. Buddhism. 2. Buddh Gaya (India) 3.
Buddha.] I. Title. II. Series.
  BQ6480 .R67 2003
  294.3′435′095412--dc21
                            2002014391

**Acknowledgments**
The Publishers would like to thank the following for permission to reproduce photographs: Associated Press
p. 20; Corbis p. 11; Corbis/Alison Wright p. 26; Corbis/Earl Kowall p. 29; Corbis/Michael S Yamashita p. 22;
Dinodia Picture Agency pp. 13, 14, 28; Dinodia Picture Agency/M Amirtham p. 7; Dinodia/R A Acharya p. 16; E
& E Picture Library/Dorothy Burrows p. 27; Herby Munasinghe pp. 12, 18, 19; Mary Evans Picture Library p. 8;
Popperfoto p. 6; Trip/A Barrett p. 9; Trip/F Good pp. 10, 17; Trip/H Rogers p. 24; Trip/J Sweeney pp. 5, 15, 25;
Trip/Resource Foto p. 23.

Cover photograph reproduced with permission of Charlie Walker Photographic.

Every effort has been made to contact copyright holders of any material reproduced in this book.
Any omissions will be rectified in subsequent printings if notice is given to the Publisher.

# Contents

Where Is Bodh Gaya?                                      4

What Did the Buddha Do at Bodh Gaya?                     6

Bodh Gaya in Ancient Times                              8

Bodh Gaya in Modern Times                              10

What Is at Bodh Gaya?                                  12

What Else Is at Bodh Gaya?                             14

What Do Pilgrims Do at Bodh Gaya?                      16

A Pilgrimage to Bodh Gaya                              18

What Did the Buddha Teach?                             20

What Festivals Do Buddhists Celebrate?                 22

What Happens in a Buddhist Temple?                     24

Where Else Do Buddhists Go on Pilgrimages?            26

Other Places of Buddhist Worship                       28

Glossary                                               30

Index                                                  32

Words printed in bold letters, **like this**, are explained in the Glossary on page 30.

# Where Is Bodh Gaya ?

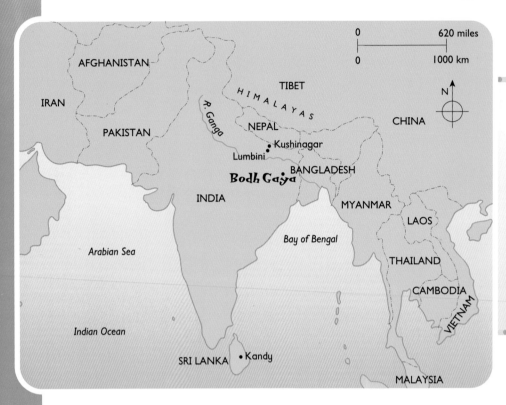

This map shows Bodh Gaya in northeast India, and the countries around it.

Bodh Gaya (say bod GAI-a) is a town in the northeast of India. Bodh Gaya is an important place for Buddhists, who follow the teachings of a holy man named the Buddha.

The Buddha was a prince who lived in India in the 6th century **B.C.E.** He wanted to understand why people were unhappy and how they could live better lives. Bodh Gaya is the place where the Buddha found understanding.

In the cool winter months, thousands of Buddhists come on a special journey, or **pilgrimage,** to Bodh Gaya. A city of tents springs up to house the **pilgrims**.

## What is Buddhism?

Buddhism is the way of life taught by the Buddha. Buddhism is different from other **religions**, because its followers do not pray to the Buddha, or treat him as a god. Instead, Buddhists try to do what is right by following the Buddha's teachings.

The Buddha taught these Four Noble Truths:
1. Life is full of suffering.
2. Suffering is caused by greed.
3. There is a way to end suffering.
4. The way to end suffering is to follow the **Middle Path** between extreme luxury and extreme hardship.

The rest of the year, when it is very hot, Bodh Gaya is a quiet place. A few tourists come to see the beautiful **temples** there and to learn about Buddhism.

Here is Bodh Gaya today. The tallest building is the Mahabodhi Temple.

# What Did the Buddha Do at Bodh Gaya?

The Buddha was a prince called Siddhattha Gotama. He grew up in a rich and comfortable palace. His father kept him away from the outside world and ordinary people. But one day, Siddhattha managed to see outside the palace. He saw that people suffered from old age, sickness, and death.

Siddhattha wanted to find out why people suffered and how they could find comfort. At first, he thought that the answer was to live very simply. He fasted for many years, which means he ate and drank very little. But he realized that this was not the answer. Instead, he decided to try **meditating.**

A Buddhist monk is meditating.

## What is meditating?

To meditate means to sit quietly and let your mind grow still, so that you feel calm and peaceful. Many Buddhists meditate every day. They believe that meditating is a way to reach Enlightenment.

Buddhists say that Enlightenment is like waking from a deep sleep and being able to see the true meaning of life. The word "Buddha" means "someone who has reached Enlightenment."

The Buddha sat quietly meditating in a village under a fig tree for a day and a night. At last he found **Enlightenment,** which means seeing things clearly, or as they really are. That tree was called the Bodhi Tree, or "tree of wisdom." The village was named Bodh Gaya after it. The Buddha spent the rest of his life as a wandering **monk.** He traveled around teaching people what he had learned.

This is a Buddhist painting showing the Buddha and his followers.

# Bodh Gaya in Ancient Times

When the Buddha was alive, 2,500 years ago, Bodh Gaya was an important place. His followers traveled there to **meditate** where the Buddha had found **Enlightenment.** Bodh Gaya grew into a busy market town. Pilgrims continued to go there after the Buddha died.

About 150 years later, a leader called Asoka ruled India. Asoka became a Buddhist. He built many Buddhist **temples** and monuments in India.

Asoka wanted to make Bodh Gaya a special place. He built a **shrine** on the site, which later became the Mahabodhi Temple. He also built a Buddhist **monastery.**

This is a painting of Asoka.

## Buddhist writings

After the Buddha died, his followers told and retold his teachings to remember them. Then, about 400 years later, his followers decided to write down his teachings.

One set of writings is called the Tipitaka. It is in a language called Pali, which the Buddha probably spoke. The main set of writings is written in Sanskrit, an ancient Indian language. Buddhists read and study these writings today.

Asoka encouraged Buddhists to go on **pilgrimages** to Bodh Gaya and other **sacred** places. Buddhists traveling on pilgrimages helped to spread Buddhism through Asia.

One important pilgrim was a Chinese Buddhist **monk** named Hiuen Tsang. He visited Bodh Gaya in the 7th century **C.E.** and collected hundreds of Buddhist prayers and poems. He spent the rest of his life **translating** them into Chinese.

Here a young boy reads a page from the Buddhist writings.

# Bodh Gaya in Modern Times

Gradually, other **religions** such as **Hinduism** and **Islam** grew more popular in India. From about the 1500s C.E., Buddhism almost disappeared there, although it was very popular in other countries. Few **pilgrims** came to Bodh Gaya anymore. Gradually, the buildings crumbled and decayed.

In the 1800s C.E., a British **archaeologist** named Alexander Cunningham rediscovered Bodh Gaya. He started to rebuild some of the **temples**.

Then, Buddhists around the world began to collect money to rebuild Bodh Gaya. They started to come on pilgrimages there once again. During the 20th century, many new temples were built at Bodh Gaya.

This shows some of the ancient temples at Bodh Gaya.

## Where do Buddhists live today?

Today, most Buddhists live in Asia, where Buddhism began. In some countries, such as Thailand and Sri Lanka, most of the people are Buddhists. There are many Buddhists in other countries in Asia, such as India, China, and Japan, but there they are not the biggest group.

In the early 20th century, some people in Europe and the United States began to follow Buddhism. Buddhism is followed in different ways in different countries, but all Buddhists share the same basic beliefs. There are now about 400 million Buddhists around the world.

Today, Bodh Gaya is a small market town. Colorful stalls line the road to the Mahabodhi Temple, selling food and souvenirs to the thousands of pilgrims who come to visit.

A stall near the Mahabodhi Temple sells souvenirs and religious pictures.

**11**

# What Is at Bodh Gaya?

At the heart of Bodh Gaya is the huge Bodhi Tree. It is a type of fig tree called a "pipal." The Buddha is said to have sat under the tree and **meditated** until he reached **Enlightenment.**

The tree there today is not the same one that the Buddha sat under, but it is a descendant of the original tree. The tree that stands there now is probably the fourth tree to have grown from seed. As each tree has died, another one has grown in its place.

The Bodhi Tree is surrounded by many beautiful Buddhist **temples.** The main one is the Mahabodhi Temple. It stands at the exact spot where the Buddha is said to have reached Enlightenment. Inside, the Mahabodhi

Pilgrims stand beneath the Bodhi Tree at Bodh Gaya.

## What is a stupa?

A stupa is a kind of Buddhist temple. Stupas were often built to mark a special place in Buddhist history. In India, the first stupas were shaped like domes. But as Buddhism spread to other countries, different shapes developed. For instance, in China and Japan, most stupas are tall and thin.

Temple is richly decorated with gold. There is a huge golden statue of the Buddha. This statue is about 1,700 years old.

At Bodh Gaya there are many other temples and stupas from the different traditions of Buddhism.

This is the Japanese Temple at Bodh Gaya.

# What Else Is at Bodh Gaya?

This picture shows the Buddha meditating under the Bodhi Tree.

The Buddha stayed at Bodh Gaya for a while after he reached **Enlightenment.** He continued **meditating** for several more weeks. Other buildings there tell the story.

For the first week after his Enlightenment, the Buddha continued to meditate under the Bodhi Tree. A throne carved out of sandstone shows the spot where he sat.

In the second week, he practiced walking meditation, which means he meditated by pacing up and down. To remember this, a path called the Jewel Walk, or the Chankramana, was built in the place where he walked. It is on a low platform, about 60 feet (18 meters) long. Carved stone **lotus** flowers mark the places where the Buddha put his feet.

## Lotus flowers

For Buddhists, the lotus flower (a kind of water lily) is a symbol of goodness and purity. Lotuses grow in the water, with their roots in the mud. But their flowers rise above the mud and the water to bloom on the surface. In the same way, people can rise above the troubles of the world and achieve Enlightenment.

For another week, the Buddha gazed at the Bodhi Tree. A **stupa** called Animesh Lochana, which means "the place of gazing without blinking" was built here.

Buddhists believe that the Buddha bathed in a lake called the Lotus Pond at Bodh Gaya. The story says that a type of snake called a cobra saved the Buddha from drowning while he was in deep meditation.

This statue of the Buddha with a cobra was built in the Lotus Pond at Bodh Gaya.

# What Do Pilgrims Do at Bodh Gaya?

At Bodh Gaya, Buddhist **pilgrims** come to visit the Bodhi Tree, the Mahabodhi **Temple,** and the other temples there. They also spend time **meditating.**

They offer gifts of flowers, candles, and **incense** to the Buddha. Incense is a kind of gum mixed with wood shavings. When it burns, it gives off a sweet-smelling smoke.

The Bodhi Tree is bright with colored threads and prayer flags tied to its branches by pilgrims. Prayer flags are little scraps of silk or other material with prayers written on them. When they wave in the wind, Buddhists believe that their prayers are being said over and over again.

Pilgrims meditate beside the Bodhi Tree.

## Gifts and symbols

Buddhists offer flowers to the Buddha as a **symbol** of life. A flower looks and smells sweet, but it will soon wilt and die. This reminds Buddhists of the teaching that nothing lasts forever.

Buddhists also light lamps and candles from the flame of another candle. This is a symbol of the light of knowledge passing from the Buddha to his followers, and from person to person.

Pilgrims also give food to the **monks** who live at Bodh Gaya. By offering these gifts, pilgrims hope to get closer to **Enlightenment**.

Candles are lit around the temples at Bodh Gaya.

# A Pilgrimage to Bodh Gaya

Herbie Munasinghe, a Buddhist from Birmingham, England, went on a **pilgrimage** to Bodh Gaya with his wife, Prema. He talks about his memories of their pilgrimage.

*We planned a trip to India to visit many of the Buddhist **sacred** places there. We flew to Delhi with a few close friends, and then we traveled overland by train and bus. It was a long journey.*

*At that time, there were thousands of Buddhist pilgrims from all over the world visiting Bodh Gaya. But still it felt calm and beautiful. We were on sacred ground, where the Buddha had trodden. It was a peaceful time, full of joy.*

Herbie and other pilgrims meditate under the Bodhi Tree.

We sat and **meditated** under the sacred Bodhi Tree right through the day, from early in the morning until darkness fell. Under the tree, I felt as though I was sitting at the Buddha's feet, learning from our great teacher. As I meditated, I thought of all the good and bad things I had done in my life. I made up my mind to try to do more good things in the future, and to avoid bad thoughts and deeds.

The next day we visited many of the **temples** at Bodh Gaya, lighting candles and laying flowers in front of the statues of the Buddha. Also, we gave money to the poor, another important teaching of the Buddha.

We brought home a small clay statue of the Buddha to keep in our home, as a reminder of our pilgrimage to Bodh Gaya.

Prema Munasinghe sits at Bodh Gaya.

19

# What Did the Buddha Teach?

The statue of the Buddha is in Chuang-Yen Monastery's Great Buddha Hall in Carmel, New York.

The Buddha taught that being born, growing old, and being **reborn** is a **cycle** that goes on and on like a wheel. The way to escape this endless cycle is to gain **Enlightenment.** Buddhists try to live good lives so that they can reach a place of peace and happiness that is called **Nirvana.** They desire to reach Nirvana very much.

The Buddha also taught that all living things are precious. Every person and animal is part of the cycle of life and rebirth. So Buddhists try to treat everyone with respect and loving kindness.

## The Three Jewels

Buddhists say that the Buddha's teachings are like jewels, because they are beautiful and precious. The Three Jewels are the three most important things for Buddhists. Every day, they say the Three Jewels aloud.

- The first jewel is the Buddha himself.
- The second jewel is the Buddha's teaching, called the Dhamma. Buddhists follow the Dhamma to try to live a good life, so that they can reach Enlightenment.
- The third jewel is the Sangha. This is the community of **monks, nuns,** and ordinary Buddhists. Remembering the Sangha helps Buddhists to look after other people. It also helps them to ignore any feelings of greed or selfishness.

## The Five Promises

The Buddha taught the Five Promises, a set of guidelines for everyday life.

- Not to harm any living thing (Because of this, many Buddhists choose not to eat meat.)
- Not to steal anything
- To be loyal in marriage
- Not to tell lies or to speak unkindly
- Not to drink alcohol or take drugs

# What Festivals Do Buddhists Celebrate?

Many Buddhist festivals are celebrated all across the world, although the celebrations are different in each country.

Wesak is celebrated in May. It is the most important festival of the year. Buddhists remember the Buddha's birth, **Enlightenment,** and death. People send Wesak cards, visit the **temple** to **meditate,** and decorate their homes with lanterns and flowers. In Thailand, Buddhists decorate the **shrines.** They pour scented water over the statues of the Buddha.

Children are pouring water over a statue of the Buddha.

## Buddha's birthday

Japanese Buddhists celebrate Hana Matsuri, the Buddha's birthday, on April 8. In the temple, scented tea is poured over a statue of the Buddha as a baby. This is to remember the Buddha's first bath, when two streams of scented water poured from the sky to wash him. The festival also celebrates the coming of spring.

Esala Perahera, the festival of the **sacred** tooth, is celebrated in Kandy, Sri Lanka. In July or August, a procession of a hundred elephants walks through the town. One elephant carries a jeweled box that holds the sacred tooth. The tooth is said to have belonged to the Buddha himself. Noisy crowds line the route, with fire eaters, dancers, and drummers.

Elephants walk in procession for Esala Perahera, the festival of the sacred tooth, in Kandy, Sri Lanka.

23

# What Happens in a Buddhist Temple?

In the **temple,** Buddhists pay their respects to Buddha. They meet there to **meditate** and hear readings from Buddha's teachings. They make offerings of flowers, candles, and **incense.** They also give money to help the needy.

There is no special day of the week when Buddhists go to the temple. But many Buddhists make a special effort to meditate and go to the temple each month at the full moon.

Every Buddhist temple contains a **shrine.** A shrine is a special place often beautifully decorated with gold, that holds a statue or a picture of the Buddha.

Young children sit at a Buddhist temple in Britain.

Buddhists sit or kneel on the floor near the shrine to meditate. They bow or put their hands together. Sometimes they lie flat on the floor. These are ways of showing respect to the Buddha.

Many Buddhists chant to help them meditate. Chanting is half-singing, half-speaking words from the scriptures. Chanting is very calming to do and to listen to.

## Prayer wheels

In some temples, especially Tibetan Buddhist temples, there are prayer wheels. A prayer wheel is a drum with a paper scroll inside. Thousands of prayers are written on the scroll. When the prayer wheel is spun, Buddhists believe that the prayers are released into the world.

This man spins Tibetan prayer wheels.

25

# Where Else Do Buddhists Go on Pilgrimages?

Lumbini, in Sarnath, Nepal, is another place of **pilgrimage** for Buddhists. The Buddha was born at Lumbini. Legend says that at the moment the Buddha was born the earth was flooded with light, and the trees all around him were covered in blossoms.

Today monks live in a **monastery** at Lumbini, and there are **temples** there where people can **meditate.** A stone there is carved with the words "Here the Buddha was born" to mark the spot.

Monks walk around the stupas at Lumbini, Nepal.

This is the stupa at Samath, where the Buddha began teaching.

After his **Enlightenment** at Bodh Gaya, the Buddha traveled to Sarnath, 217 miles (350 kilometers) away. He gave his first teaching in a park there. To explain his teaching, he drew a wheel on the ground. This showed the endless cycle of life, death, and rebirth in which everyone is caught up.

A **stupa** was built on the spot where the Buddha is believed to have taught about his beliefs for the very first time. Pilgrims walk three times around the stupa in a clockwise direction, once for each of the Three Jewels. You can read about the Three Jewels on page 21.

### Walking clockwise

Pilgrims walk clockwise around the stupa at Sarnath because they believe they should move around the Buddha in the same way that the planets move around the Sun. They also chant the sacred phrase *Om mani padme hum*, or "Praise to the jewel in the **lotus.**"

# Other Places of Buddhist Worship

The third-holiest Buddhist spot is Kushinagar, in north India. Many Buddhists make **pilgrimages** to the **stupa** in Kushinagar. The Buddha left his body here at the age of 80. (Buddhists prefer to say "left his body" rather than died.) Some statues of the Buddha show him lying on his side, because this is how he left his body. Legend says that an earthquake shook the Earth when the Buddha left his body, as it had when he was born and when he first achieved **Enlightenment**.

This is the statue of the Buddha lying on his side at Kushinagar.

As well as going to the **temple** or on pilgrimage, Buddhists can **meditate** and read the Buddha's teachings at home.

Many Buddhists have a **shrine** in their home. It may be a room, or part of a room, with a small statue of the Buddha. Every day, members of the family may meditate beside the shrine, and read or chant from the Buddhist writings. They may offer flowers, candles, and **incense** to the statue of the Buddha.

This boy and his family are at a Buddhist temple in Hong Kong.

# Glossary

**archaeologist**   someone who studies how people lived in the past by digging up land or old buildings

**B.C.E.**   stands for Before the Common Era. People of all religions can use this, rather than the Christian B.C. that counts up to the birth of Jesus. The year numbers are not changed.

**C.E.**   stands for the Common Era, now used instead of the Christian A.D. The year numbers are not changed.

**cycle**   pattern that goes around and around without stopping, like a wheel turning

**Enlightenment**   understanding the truth about the way things really are

**Hinduism**   religion followed by Hindu people. Hindus worship many gods.

**incense**   substance that is burned to make sweet-smelling smoke. Incense can be made from spices or special types of wood.

**Islam**   religion followed by Muslims

**lotus**   another name for a water lily flower

**meditate (meditation)**   way of controlling your mind so that you can relax and concentrate

**Middle Path**   not having too much or too little of anything. Buddhists believe that following the Middle Path helps them to overcome greed and desire, which cause unhappiness, and so reach Enlightenment.

**monastery**   place where monks and nuns live, and other people may come to study

**monk**   man who has chosen to make religion the most important thing in his life

**nun**   woman who has chosen to make religion the most important thing in her life

**Nirvana**   a state of perfect peace and happiness that Buddhists wish to reach

**pilgrimage**   journey made for religious reasons

**pilgrim**   someone who goes on a pilgrimage

**reborn**   to be born again. Buddhists believe that all living creatures must die and be reborn until they reach Enlightenment.

**religion**   belief in God or gods

**sacred**   holy, or to do with holy things

**shrine**   special place for meditation or religious worship. A shrine can be in a  temple or at home.

**stupa**   Buddhist temple built to mark a sacred spot or hold a sacred object

**symbol**   picture or sign that stands for something else

**temple**   place of worship or religious building

**translating**   changing words or writing from one language into another

# Index

Animesh Lochana 15
Asoka 8, 9

Bodh Gaya 4–5, 8–9, 10–19
Bodhi Tree 7, 12, 14, 15, 16
Buddha 4, 5, 6–7, 8, 12–13,
    14–15, 23, 26, 27, 28
Buddhism 4, 5, 10, 11
Buddhist teachings 5, 20–21
Buddhist writings 9, 29

chanting 25, 29
cycle of rebirth 20, 27

Dhamma 21

Enlightenment 7, 8, 12, 15, 17, 20,
    22, 28
Esala Perahera 23

fasting 6
festivals 22–23
Five Promises 21
Four Noble Truths 5
Hana Matsuri 23
Hinduism 10
Hiuen Tsang 9

incense 16, 29
Islam 10

Jewel Walk 14

Kushinagar 28

lotus flowers 14, 15
Lotus Pond 15
Lumbini 26

Mahabodhi Temple 5, 8, 12–13
meditation 6–7, 8, 12, 14, 16, 19,
    24, 25, 26, 29
Middle Path 5
monasteries 8, 26
monks and nuns 7, 9, 17, 21, 26

Nirvana 20

pilgrimage 4, 8, 9, 10, 16–19,
    26–28
prayer flags and wheels 16, 17,
    25
Sangha 21
Sarnath 27
shrines 8, 22, 24, 29
stupas 13, 15, 27, 28

temples 5, 8, 12–13, 16, 22,
    24–25, 26
Three Jewels 21, 27
Tipitaka 9

Wesak 22